JavaScript:

*Tips and Tricks
to Programming Code
with JavaScript*

Charlie Masterson

Table of Contents

Introduction

JavaScript, a widely used programming language is an integral part of a web programmer's life and programming skills. It is the foundation of what makes web pages interactive and dynamic; it's used to create forms, polls, and quizzes and is often used in lightweight programming.

It's the most common computer language utilized in all major browsers from the humble Internet Explorer to the advanced Google Chrome and Safari. Most computers already come with JavaScript installed into their system, so it's guaranteed that visitors from all around the world will be able to view what you have on the internet, software and computer programs.

Everyone and anyone can use JavaScript without purchasing licenses.

Also, in case you are wondering, JavaScript and Java are completely two different computer languages used for various programming needs.

The thing about JavaScript is that there are plenty of JavaScript codes pre-written that you can copy and plug it directly into your web page for a similar effect, instead of writing all the codes again on your own. All you every need to know is find out what the code does and then where to copy and paste these codes in its particular places to get the desired effect, like baking a cake.

If you have opened this book, we are not going to go into the specifics of JavaScript and teach you the basics or the steps of coding and programming or pasting these codes into your web page.

What this book will do however, is give you loads of tips and tricks to help you navigate your way into becoming a better programmer and use JavaScript more efficiently.

A Brief History of JavaScript

Back in the 1990s when the world wide web was still in its developing stages, all web pages were static- there was no way of interaction between user and the website. What you saw was exactly what was set up.

Two of the most popular browsers at that time were Internet Explorer and Netscape Navigator. While the Internet Explorer was a lot more famous, Netscape was the first to bring about a programming language that enabled a webpage to be interactive with the user. This language was called LiveScript and it was integrated into Netscape's browsers. Anyone using Netscape could now interact with the pages thanks to this language. LiveScript did not need a plugin.

On another note, there was another programming language that required a separate plugin to run and that was called Java. At this point, Java became very well known and Netscape decided to cash in on this by renaming LiveScript to JavaScript.

As mentioned earlier, there is a wide difference between Java and JavaScript, although their codes appear similar.

And then Internet Explorer, with the need to innovate, is updated and supported by two integrated languages which was called vbscript based on BASIC programming and another called Jscript which was similar to JavaScript.

By the time Internet Explore became the most used browser, JavaScript also became the most accepted and widely used programming language to be used in up and coming web browsers.

Fast forward to 1996, scripting language became so important that it was risky to leave it to competing browser developers. In that same year, JavaScript was given to the ECMA, the international standards body who was responsible for the development of programming language. This language was officially renamed to ECMAScript but programmers and everyone else still know it as JavaScript.

It's a lot cooler sounding too.

The Importance of JavaScript

To understand how JavaScript is used is to understand the basic roles of other programming that goes into the development of a webpage.

Simply put:

1- HTML is the language that is used to markup content. HTML defines what the content is, and not how it looks on a webpage.

2- CSS is used to define the appearance of a webpage. This entails specifying which media corresponds to which command

Just by using these two languages, you can already create a static webpage that can be easily accessed regardless of what device you view the webpage on and what browser is used to access it.

However, the biggest disadvantage of web pages like these is that the only way your visitor can interact with your static site is by filling up a form and waiting for a new page to load.

That's where JavaScript comes in.

JavaScript converts static pages into one that is interactive so that site visitors won't need to wait for a new page to load every time they make a request. JavaScript enables your web pages to have a behavior - to make them capable of responding to a variety of actions in real-time.

With JavaScript, you can:

- Validate each field in a form as a user enters the information and not fill up the whole form and only be told the user made a typo after submitting the form.

- Enables your page to be interactive in more ways than involving forms
- Add animations to a page, attracting attention to a specific part or making the website easier to use
- Load new and heavier images and scripts on the webpage
- Enables you to improve your visitor's experiences

Chapter 1:
Simple Tricks to
Help You
Learn JavaScript
Faster

Oftentimes when anyone is on the path of learning JavaScript or any coding skill, they often experience some of these issues:

- Confusing concepts
- Time and motivation to learn
- Easy to forget codes
- Tooling landscape keeps changing

In this chapter, we are going to look at conquering these challenges with some mind tricks that can help you learn the JavaScript landscape faster, making you a more productive coder.

TIP 1: CREATE A ROADMAP OF WHAT YOU WANT TO LEARN

Let's face it- there are plenty of frameworks to use and new coders are always at the crossroads of which to start off with first. Instead of researching which frameworks to start on, one of the best ways to overcome this would be to create your roadmap of learning what you need to know.

For example, if you want to become a front-end developer, then your roadmap could look like this:

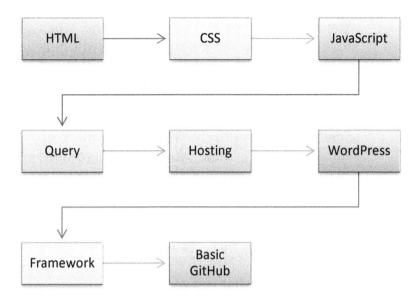

HTML and CSS are the most basic coding knowledge you need to know before you proceed to learn other things. Then you can move on to JavaScript and jQuery. Once you have created your roadmap, it'll make it easier for you to focus on what is essential first so you don't waste time and effort.

TIP 2: TAKE YOUR TIME

Wanting to understand coding quickly will be one of the harmful things that can halt your progress of learning coding and JavaScript.

Attempting to skim something and then moving on to the next issue at hand will only make you forget things even more. You'll forget what you read the first time, go back to it and read it to refresh your memory and then move on. By this time, you'd have forgotten something else entirely. This cycle will keep repeating, and then you'll find yourself discouraged. To prevent this from happening, you can do this:

- Limit the amount of coding to a particular task. Learn one thing at a time
- Practice what you've learned

By learning and practicing your coding skills, you'll find that it is a lot easier to remember things and absorb them as you go on learning new things. This process may seem longer, but practice does make it perfect.

TIP 3: PRACTICE WITH THE RIGHT MINDSET

Remember this: if you try to take shortcuts in your JavaScript practice, you will only end up taking a longer time to learn it. Yes practicing is boring and repetitive but here are some ways to make it exciting:

Try treating each new concept in JavaScript like a new toy, car or iPhone or even a new dress. You are excited to try it, especially when it's new and you use it several times. Apply something cool with the concept that you've just learned; surprise yourself and show your friends your new skill.

With a slightly more playful approach to learning new things, you can have fun while learning. You'll also find that you remember these concepts longer and you learn a lot faster.

TIP 4: COMPARTMENTALIZING YOUR TIME

Finding time to practice coding can be difficult. However, the same people who code are also heavy social media users, often spending time on YouTube and Facebook, Reddit or even Wikipedia. Whether or not you are like this, there are valuable lessons to be learned from using social media.

The fact that we all spend so much time on Facebook even if all we just wanted to do was just to look at one notification says a lot. We get sucked into Facebook because one thing leads to another and because you constantly have people updating their status and walls and your news feed always have something new to see.

Using this same psychology, you can use this to your advantage in learning code. Instead of committing several hours of learning codes, you can just tell yourself that you will commit to 15 whole minutes without any disturbance.

Then look at Facebook, take a little break.

Then come back again and do another 15 minutes.

But, this technique can only work if stay focused to your goal, and not allow Facebook or anything other suck you into, and make you totally forget what you were doing.

TIP 5: GIVE YOURSELF TIME

There's a saying that goes if you take your time to think slowly, you'll learn a lot faster. Coding needs time. You need time to understand it. Otherwise, you'll only get more confused. Take your time to figure out what it is that you are trying to learn. Explain it to someone if you have to. Take your time to go through each step, and each line of code before you figure it all in one go.

TIP 6: WRITE IN PLAIN LANGUAGE

Coding can be incredibly complex. If what you are reading becomes too complicated or unfamiliar, then try writing it out in simple terms- or in any way that you can understand it first. That way, you can figure out what it is that you want to code before actually writing it.

This will enable you to code much easily the next time around, and you'll also be faster at writing your codes because you wouldn't need to stop and think with each line of code. You'll also be able to spot bugs even before you code them in.

BOTTOM LINE

Many of these tips can make you learn JavaScript easily and at a faster rate. The truth is, you would be able to apply these tips to learn any sort of lesson you need to.

Chapter 2: JavaScript Cheat Sheet – Must Haves for Every Programmer

By now you know how important learning JavaScript is if you are serious about becoming a programmer. JavaScript is no doubt the most practical programming language in our digital world. It is used in app development, web apps, web pages and programming in general.

In this chapter, we introduce to you some of the must-have cheat sheets you can get your hands on to make yourself better at coding and writing the programming language. These cheat sheets are handy to have as they help you master the basics while you are learning.

CHEATOGRAPHY JAVASCRIPT CHEAT SHEET

With this site, you can find various listing methods and functions that include guides to common expressions as well as more complicated items such as the XMLHttpRequest object as well as many references to JavaScript.

QUICKLYCODE- PROGRAMMING CHEAT SHEET AND MANY OTHERS

This site links you to even more cheat sheets and other resources for your programming needs from JavaScript to SQL, Java, WordPress, Ruby on Rails and PHP.

FIRSTSITEGUIDE JAVASCRIPT CHEAT SHEET

FirstSiteGuide comprises several self-confessed web geeks who offer advice and tutorials on everything from SEO to marketing, web hosting, design and development. They also link you up to free resources and toolkits.

MOOTOOLS CHEAT SHEET

This site gives you all kinds of JavaScript utilities that are excellent for JavaScript developers in the intermediate or advanced levels. You can write powerful and flexible coding with the many well documented and elegant APIs.

A COMPACT JAVASCRIPT FRAMEWORK

jQUERY CHEATSHEET

Managed by Oscar Otero, the jQUERY Cheat Sheet enables developers to find functions and properties related to jQuery 1.3 library.

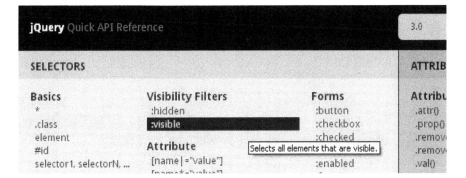

STEAMFEED HTML & JAVASCRIPT SHORTCUTS

The good people at SteamFeed came up with a great cheat sheet that puts HTML codes and JavaScript information in a clean and easily readable infographic that you can print and place at reading distance so you have easy access when practicing your coding.

WEB DESIGN CHEAT SHEET

If you need a site that you can go to for all sorts of cheat sheets related to web design, then Sellfy has some good resources for CSS, responsive web design cheat sheets, HTML tags and many more.

29 Must-Have Cheat Sheets for Web Designers

By Yuri Burchenya
December 9, 2014

Facebook   Twitter   Google+

29 MUST-HAVE CHEAT SHEETS

THE ULTIMATE JAVASCRIPT CHEAT SHEET

This cheat list from the website codementor, offers a quick overview of the JavaScript language. You have the choice to either read it from the start or to jump to a topic that you like.

The Ultimate JavaScript Cheat Sheet

Chapter 3:
Tips and Tricks to Design and Build Your Own JavaScript Library

JavaScript Library you say?

No, it doesn't contain books. It does, however, include packaged codes that web designers, developers, and programmers can use in their projects that will save time and effort. In other words, you do not need to reinvent the wheel when you want to apply the same package of codes to deliver the same kind of effect on different websites and programs.

So what makes a JavaScript Library?

Here are a few distinct features of a JavaScript Library:

- It has one file or several files in a single folder

- Its coding must be maintained separately and remain as-is when you use it to implement a project

- It should allow the user to set project-specific behavior or configuration

In this chapter, we will talk about why you should build a JavaScript library and how they are built- in the simplest ways possible.

Why build your own JavaScript Library?

Firstly, it makes things convenient for programmers and web developers alike, especially if you code and develop plenty of programs, websites, and web applications. Having a library with existing codes makes your job easier and saves you time since you do not need to keep digging up old projects from some obscure folder in your hard drive. All you just need to is pull it out of your library. You have a convenient place to store all your codes; you have a place to fragment all your applications and keep them all in an easier to maintain location.

Essentially, any code that makes your work easier and which can be reused is a great component to be added to the library. One such good example is jQuery. jQuery's API is a more simplified DOM API. Back when cross-browser DOM manipulation was difficult, jQuery was essential.

And if an open-source venture becomes increasingly popular, more developers use it, and it will eventually encourage more developers to join in and assist with this venture by contributing to the code and submitting issues that will help make it easier to manipulate. This contribution will benefit the library and all other experiments that depend on it.

Popular open-source projects can also lead to fantastic opportunities for developers alike. A tech firm or any organization may be impressed by the quality of a developer's work, and they will be offered a job. It could also mean that a company will provide a developer to collaborate on a project or get them to integrate their project into an application of their own.

But for most developers or coders, having their own library is a hobby; one that enables them to write multiple codes and help others and contribute to the process.

Your Goals and Scope of Work

Before you set out writing your codes, you need to be clear on what your goals are for this library. With this, it will help you keep focused on what problems you encounter and how to solve them with your library.

Your primary goal is also to make your library easy to use. Essentially, the simpler your API, the easier it will be for anyone to use your library.

So ask yourself- what problems does your library solve and how can you solve it? Will you utilize codes from someone else's library or will you write everything yourself?

In chapter 1, we discussed creating a roadmap. This roadmap for your library will be one of the techniques you use in any other code development you set out to do.

A Roadmap for your library:

-      List out the features you want in your library

-   Make these features minimum and practical

-   Create milestones for each feature

What you are doing with the roadmap is setting goals for each function, essentially breaking your project into manageable sizes so it is easier to accomplish and the process of creating it is a lot more enjoyable. It'll also keep you sane and focused.

Your Library API Design

When creating your library, think of yourself as the end-user. By putting yourself as the user, you will work towards a user-centric design and development. This will make your library more convenient to use by anyone who has access to it.

Testing Your API

The best way to test the quality of your API is to use it for your projects. What you can do is to substitute the application code with your library and see if the result it gives covers all the features you want. Keep to the minimum bare essentials as possible and also provide room for flexibility to change and revise anything that may seem slightly off.

Here is one example of what the implementation coding or User-Agent string library outline would look like:

Code:

```
// Start with empty UserAgent string
var userAgent = new UserAgent;

// Create and add first product:
EvilCorpBrowser/1.2 (X11; Linux; en-us)
var application = new
UserAgent.Product('EvilCorpBrowser',
'1.2');
application.setComment('X11', 'Linux',
'en-us');
userAgent.addProduct(application);

// Create and add second product:
Blink/20420101
var engine = new
UserAgent.Product('Blink', '20420101');
userAgent.addProduct(engine);
```

```
// EvilCorpBrowser/1.2 (X11; Linux; en-
us) Blink/20420101
userAgent.toString();

// Make some more changes to engine
product
engine.setComment('Hello World');

// EvilCorpBrowser/1.2 (X11; Linux; en-
us) Blink/20420101 (Hello World)
userAgent.toString();
```

Depending on how complex your library is, you also need to give some thought to structuring. One way to do this is to utilize design patterns to structure your library as well as overcome any technical issues you may experience along the way.

Structuring also reduces the risk of re-aligning huge parts when you are adding new features to your library.

Flexibility and Customization

A cool thing about most JavaScript libraries out there is its flexibility. However, many developers face problems when deciding what they can and cannot customize. One of this is the chart.js and D3.js.

Both elements are great libraries to visualize data. If you need more control over your graphics, then the D3.js is what you want. If you want something that is easy to create yet give you different types of built-in charts, then Chart.js is the one to use.

There are three ways that you can give your user control over your library:

1- Configuration

2- Exposing public methods

3- Callbacks & events

Configuring a library is often done at the project initialization stage, but some of these libraries also allow you to set during run-time. These configurations are commonly limited to simple issues as changing these settings will only update these values for use later on.

Code:

```
// Configure at initialization

var userAgent = new UserAgent({
  commentSeparator: ';'
});

// Run-time configuration using a public
method
userAgent.setOption('commentSeparator',
'-');

// Run-time configuration using a public
property
userAgent.commentSeparator = '-';
```

Certain methods are exposed intentionally to interact with an instance (getters) such as to retrieve data from the instance or to put data in the instance (setters) as well as perform certain actions.

Code:

```
var userAgent = new UserAgent;

// A getter to retrieve comments from all
products
userAgent.getComments();

// An action to shuffle the order of all
products
userAgent.shuffleProducts();
```

Callbacks are also sometimes accepted and passed using public methods and it often used to run user-codes after an asynchronous task.

```
var userAgent = new UserAgent;

userAgent.doAsyncThing(function
asyncThingDone() {
   // Run code after async thing is done
});
```

Events have a huge potential in JavaScript libraries. Slightly similar to callbacks, they have a slight difference where adding event handlers do not cause trigger actions. Events are also used to indicate certain events and can provide additional information to the user as well as return a specific value for the library to correspond with.

Code:

```
var userAgent = new UserAgent;

// Validate a product on addition
userAgent.on('product.add', function
onProductAdd(e, product) {
  var shouldAddProduct =
product.toString().length < 5;

  // Tell the library to add the product
or not
  return shouldAddProduct;
});
```

You may also enable your users to extend your own library. In order to do this, you need to make available your public method or property so that users can populate it, such as the Angular modules.

Code:

```
(angular.module('myModule')) and

jQuery's fn(jQuery.fn.myPlugin)
```

You can also just do nothing of the above and allow users to access your library through its namespace.

Code:

```javascript
// AngryUserAgent module
// Has access to UserAgent namespace
(function AngryUserAgent(UserAgent) {

  // Create new method .toAngryString()
  UserAgent.prototype.toAngryString =
function() {
    return this.toString().toUpperCase();
  };

})(UserAgent);

// Application code
var userAgent = new UserAgent;
// ...

// EVILCORPBROWSER/1.2 (X11; LINUX; EN-
US) BLINK/20420101
userAgent.toAngryString();
```

Similarly, this allows you to overwrite
methods as well.

```javascript
// AngryUserAgent module
(function AngryUserAgent(UserAgent) {

  // Store old .toString() method for
later use
  var _toString =
UserAgent.prototype.toString;

  // Overwrite .toString()
  UserAgent.prototype.toString =
function() {
    return
_toString.call(this).toUpperCase();
  };

})(UserAgent);

var userAgent = new UserAgent;
// ...

// EVILCORPBROWSER/1.2 (X11; LINUX; EN-
US) BLINK/20420101
```

```
userAgent.toString();
```

In this case, giving users access to your library's namespace also gives you less control over how plugins and extensions are defined.

To allow for extensions to follow some certain convention, you need to write documentation.

Testing

For test-driven development, an outline is essential. In other words, this is the time when you write down the features and criteria in the form of tests, even before you write down the actual library.

If your test show you that a feature behaves like it was supposed to, and you write it down before writing it in your library, then this strategy is called behavior-driven development.

If your tests cover every aspect of your library then and if your code surpasses all these tests, then you can safely say that your library is working well.

Other testing frameworks that you can use are:

Unit Test Your JavaScript by Mocha and Chai by Jani Hartikainen, where you can write unit tests in Mocha.

Testing JavaScript with Jasmine, Travis, and Karma by Tim Evko shows you how to set up a testing pipeline coherently with another framework called Jasmine.

Below mentioned is another outline that you can try by Tim Severien. He has used a Jasmine test for his library and it looks something like this.

Code:

```javascript
describe('Basic usage', function () {
  it('should generate a single product',
function () {
    // Create a single product
    var product = new
UserAgent.Product('EvilCorpBrowser',
'1.2');
    product.setComment('X11', 'Linux',
'en-us');

    expect(product.toString())
      .toBe('EvilCorpBrowser/1.2 (X11;
Linux; en-us)');
  });

  it('should combine several products',
function () {
    var userAgent = new UserAgent;

    // Create and add first product
    var application = new
UserAgent.Product('EvilCorpBrowser',
'1.2');
    application.setComment('X11',
'Linux', 'en-us');
    userAgent.addProduct(application);

    // Create and add second product
```

```
    var engine = new
UserAgent.Product('Blink', '20420101');
    userAgent.addProduct(engine);

    expect(userAgent.toString())
      .toBe('EvilCorpBrowser/1.2 (X11;
Linux; en-us) Blink/20420101');
  });

  it('should update products correctly',
function () {
    var userAgent = new UserAgent;

    // Create and add first product
    var application = new
UserAgent.Product('EvilCorpBrowser',
'1.2');
    application.setComment('X11',
'Linux', 'en-us');
    userAgent.addProduct(application);

    // Update first product
    application.setComment('X11',
'Linux', 'nl-nl');

    expect(userAgent.toString())
      .toBe('EvilCorpBrowser/1.2 (X11;
Linux; nl-nl)');
  });
});
```

Once you have done your testing and you are
completely satisfied with the API design for
your first library version, then you can start
thinking about the site's architecture and how
exactly will your library be used.

Module Loader Compatibility

Not many developers use module loaders, and this is entirely up to you too. However, you need to be aware that some developers that use your library might choose to use a module loader, so you need to make your library compatible with this feature.

You can choose some of the popular module loaders such as AMD, RequireJS, and CommonJS. If choosing between these functions is hard for you, you can also try Universal Module Definition (UMD) which is aimed at supporting several types of module loaders.

To make your library UMD compatible, you can also find some variations such as the UMD GitHub repository. Begin to create your library by using one of these templates. Another tip is to use Babel to compile ES5 combined with Babel's UMD plugin if you choose to use ES2015 import/export syntax function. This way, you can use ES2015 in your projects as well as produce a library that can be used by all kinds of developers using various modules.

Documentation

You need to start your documentation with basic information such as your project name as well as a short description of what it is about. This will help others understand what your library is meant to do and whether using your library is a good choice for them. You can also include a little bit more information on things such as scope and goals so users are better informed. Your roadmap can also be included so users know what they can expect in the future in your library development and how they can also contribute to it.

API, Tutorials and Examples
API documentation is also an essential part of documentation as it will tell users how exactly to use your library. Other good additions would be examples as well as tutorials. This can take up some time so you can do this as you library development is on-going.

Meta-tasks
Users will also want to make changes to your library and this is usually in the form of a contribution but some may want to create a custom build only for private use. For these users, you can include documentation for meta-tasks that include a list of commands to build the library, run testing, generate and convert or download data.

Contribution
Contributions are great especially when you open-source your library. Another

documentation you can add in is to guide contributors to explain the steps in making a contribution to the library and what kind of criteria should they fill before making a contribution. This will make your review process easier to accept contributions that can actively upgrade and enhance your library.

License

Licenses are important too. Include licenses so everyone knows what material is copyrighted. ChooseALicense.com is recommended as an excellent resource for acquiring a license without any legal advisor. Save your chosen license as text in a LICENSE.txt file format in your project's root.

Adding Versions/Releases to Your Git Repository

Versioning is necessary for a good library. The current standard for version naming is via the SemVer, short for Semantic Versioning. This version comprises three numbers to indicate different changes for major, minor and patch. If you do have a git repository, you can also add in version numbers. Consider the snapshots of your repository or Tags. To create a tag, open its terminal and do the following:

```
# git tag -a [version] -m [version
message]
git tag -a v1.2.0 -m "Awesome Library
v1.2.0"
```

GitHub for example provides a comprehensive view of all your versions as well as download links for each one of them.

Publishing to Common Repositories

npm

Most programming languages are equipped with package managers or they at least have a third party package manager that enables users to pull in specific libraries for that specific programming language. For example, PHP's manager is <u>Composer</u> and Ruby on Rails is <u>RubyGems</u>. For a standalone JavaScript engine such as Node.js you have <u>npm</u>. By default, your npm package will be available publicly. But you also have the option of publishing the following:

- <u>private packages</u>
- <u>set up a private registry</u>
- <u>completely avoid publishing</u>

However, should you decide to publish your package, then you need the package.json file. You can do this manually or use an interactive wizard for this. To begin this wizard, start by typing:

```
npm init
```

The version property should match your git tag. Include the README.md file as well. Just like

GitHub, npm uses that for the page presenting your package.

Once done, publish your package by typing:

```
npm publish
```

That's it! You have successfully published your

npm package.

Bower

Another useful package manager called Bower surfaced a few years ago. This is a package manager designed for the web. Here, you can find all major front-end asserts. The only thing is, your library will benefit from using Bower to publish your package is if your library set up to be browser-compatible.

npm packages are primarily for JavaScript and many front-end packages still use npm but Bower is still fundamentally popular so go ahead and publish using Bower too.

To generate a bower.json file, type:

```
bower init
```

Just like npm init, the instructions are self-explanatory. Finally, to publish your package:

```
bower register awesomelib
https://github.com/you/awesomelib
```

Now you have your library available for everyone to use in their Node projects or on the web!

Conclusion

Remember that your code development is the library. Make sure your library solves a problem, it is convenient and easy to use and above all stable. This will ensure that you and many other developers who use it are happy.

The tasks explained above are easily automated such as running tests and creating tags, updating your versions and publishing your packages.

Chapter 4:
JavaScript Tips &
Tricks
to Keep and
Remember

In this chapter, we will look into some short and useful tips related to improving your JavaScript skills and enhancing your code writing.

USING === Instead of ==	The == (or !=) operator performs an automatic type conversion if needed. The === (or !==) operator will not perform any conversion.
	What it will do is compare the value and the type, which could be considered faster (jsPref) than ==.

```
[10] ==  10      // is true
[10] === 10      // is false

'10' ==  10      // is true
'10' === 10      // is false

 []  ==  0       // is true
 []  === 0       // is false

 ''      ==  false   // is true
but true == "a" is false
 ''      === false   // is false
```

charAt() Shorthand	To do this, you can utilize the eval() function however this bracket notation shorthand technique is much simpler than an evaluation
	Longhand:
| | ```
"myString".charAt(0);
``` |
| | Shorthand: |
| | ```
"myString"[0]; // Returns 'm'
``` |

Strings convert to Numbers	The fastest and easiest (jsPerf) way to do this would be using the + (plus) operator.
| | ```
var one = '1';
``` |
| | ```
var numberOne = +one; // Number 1
``` |
| | You can also use the - (minus) operator which type-converts the value into number but also negates it. |
| | ```
var one = '1';
``` |
| | ```
var negativeNumberOne = -one; // Number -1
``` |
| Truthy/falsy values | You can convert a Truthy or Falsy value to true boolean with '!!' |

| converted to boolean | ```
!!"" // false
!!0 // false
!!null // false
!!undefined // false
!!NaN // false

!!"hello" // true
!!1 // true
!!{} // true
!![] // true
``` |
| Using JSON.Stringify | Let's say there is an object with properties "prop1", "prop2", "prop3". **Additional params can be passed to JSON.stringify** to selectively write properties of the object to string like:<br><br>```
var obj = {
    'prop1': 'value1',
    'prop2': 'value2',
    'prop3': 'value3'
};

var selectedProperties =
['prop1', 'prop2'];

var str = JSON.stringify(obj,
selectedProperties);

// str
//
{"prop1":"value1","prop2":"val
ue2"}
```<br><br>The **"str"** will contain only info on selected properties only. Instead of array we can pass a function also.<br><br>```
function
``` |
```

| | ```
selectedProperties(key, val) {
    // the first val will be
the entire object, key is
empty string
    if (!key) {
        return val;
    }

    if (key === 'prop1' || key
=== 'prop2') {
        return val;
    }

    return;
}
``` |
| | The last optional param it takes is to modify the way it writes the `object to string`.<br>```
var str = JSON.stringify(obj,
selectedProperties, '\t\t');

/* str output with double tabs
in every line.
{
        "prop1": "value1",
        "prop2": "value2"
}
*/
``` |
| Single Method for Arrays and Writing Single Element | Instead of writing separate methods to hold an array and a single element parameter, you can write functions so that they can handle both.<br>You just have to concat everything into an array first. Array.concat will accept an array or a single element.<br><br>```
function printUpperCase(words)
{
    var elements =
``` |
```

	``
[].concat(words || []);
  for (var i = 0; i <
elements.length; i++) {

console.log(elements[i].toUppe
rCase());
  }
}
```

Print UpperCase is now ready to accept a single node or an array of nodes as its parameter. It also avoids the potentialTypeError that would be thrown if no parameter was passed.

```
printUpperCase("cactus");
// => CACTUS
printUpperCase(["cactus",
"bear", "potato"]);
// => CACTUS
//   BEAR
//   POTATO
``` |
| Measure performance for a JavaScript Block | For quickly measuring performance of a JavaScript block, we can use the console functions like console.time(label) andconsole.timeEnd(label)

```
console.time("Array
initialize");
var arr = new Array(100),
    len = arr.length,
  i;
for (i = 0; i < len; i++) {
    arr[i] = new Object();
};
console.timeEnd("Array
initialize"); // Outputs:
Array initialize: 0.711ms
``` |
```

| Hoisting | Hoisting will help you manage your function scope. Variable declarations and functions are hoisted to the top where as variable definitions are not. |

```
function doTheThing() {
  // ReferenceError: notDeclared is
not defined
  console.log(notDeclared);

  // Outputs: undefined
  console.log(definedLater);
  var definedLater;

  definedLater = 'I am defined!'
  // Outputs: 'I am defined!'
  console.log(definedLater)

  // Outputs: undefined

console.log(definedSimulateneously);
  var definedSimulateneously = 'I am
defined!'
  // Outputs: 'I am defined!'

console.log(definedSimulateneously)

  // Outputs: 'I did it!'
  doSomethingElse();

  function doSomethingElse(){
    console.log('I did it!');
  }

  // TypeError: undefined is not a
```

|  | ```
function
  functionVar();

var functionVar = function(){
  console.log('I did it!');
}
``` |
```

Chapter 5: JavaScript Skills to Know Moving Forward

Whether you like it or not, as a programmer or web or app developer, you need to learn JavaScript. It is considered the computer language of the future simply because it is an integral part of web ad app development.

As common as it is, JavaScript is pretty complicated especially when trends keep changing and with that, comes the ensuing chaos. Despite all that, things are improving in the JavaScript landscape, and with technology evolving, old problems with JavaScript are fixed, no doubt with new ones coming in.

If you are a new developer in 2016, your willingness and ability to learn JavaScript will definitely contribute to the success of your career and your skills as a programmer/coder/hacker or developer.

So what are the trends of JavaScript development should programmers work on going forward?

In this chapter, we will look at the various things that will go big in the programming language world.

React & Redux

In 2015, React gained traction especially when more and more programmers started complaining about the AngularJS framework as 2014 came to an end. The fact that news broke out that Angular 2 will be unsuitable to run with Angular 1 made it even worse for the Angular community. React came in and closed this gap in 2016.

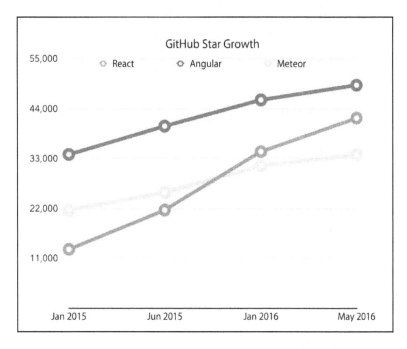

Estimates based on screenshots from the internet archive. Perhaps a more telling pointer would be the npm download count for react, angular, and Angular2 packages:

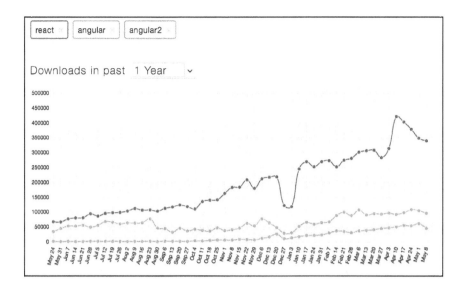

For the past year, React has been getting more traction from the JavaScript community than AngularJS has. So if you look at the graph above, you are probably wondering what happened after August? It shows that npm downloads for React have surged significantly and it also shows exactly when GitHub stars for React being to catch up with AngularJS's stars.

The change is due to Redux, created by Dan Abramov during the ReactEurope2015 conference. Redux had a simple flux implementation that convinced many programmers that it was time to adopt the one and only React.

Before the materialization of Redux, React was turbulent as people were trying to figure out how to best execute the 'Flux' architecture. Since then, many other implementations begin surfacing, and while they aren't bad, they weren't exactly solving any issues that made most JavaScript developers wary.

In spite of the universal rendering and the gold stars for React and its virtual DOM, programmers were still cautious about using it in their projects. Despite this, more and more people started using Redux and realized it makes testing and debugging apps running on JavaScript a lot easier. From then on, Redux rose from the Flux are the real winner.

React, and Redux definitely is the hottest trend for 2016, and it doesn't look like it'll fade away come 2017, regarding front-end 'framework' JavaScript. Netflix, Yahoo!, and Dropbox have all adopted React into their tech arsenal, giving it a confidence boost. Even so, Facebook's Relay looks like a prospective contender in 2017.

Other Frameworks of Interest

Other frameworks may come into the foray and while they aren't comparable but here's a general overview of what other frameworks are out there. Again, things may change with anything regarding technology. What may not work so well this year might end up becoming top of the league the next year.

Without further ado, here are some other frameworks to look into.

Angular2

Plenty of non-tech companies will be looking into using Angular 2 especially businesses that use Microsoft's.NET framework. Angular 2, developed through a partnership between Google and Microsoft was designed to make JavaScript a more manageable language.

Microsoft themselves were pushing for the.NET aggressively last year as it open-sourced quite some elements and strove to make Microsoft tools more accessible to developers. After the rewrite, the teams hope to fix any sort of escalating issues with the Angular 1 apps, and performance so far has been stellar. Angular2 has been developed to support web components, and according to Google, it is the future for web development. The AngularJS community though has differing opinions about the direction that Angular is taking- all this despite the efforts the Angular team has been investing in helping developers transition properly from Angular 1 to Angular 2.

This rewrite has also allowed React to develop and mature as with its community growing larger each day. Because of this, programmers are skeptical that Angular 2 will be as successful as Angular 1. However, as mentioned above, things can change in the tech world so it could be Angular 2 will have room to grow in 2017. Angular2 is still preferred as an alternative to the React app.

Meteor

Another upcoming trend to look out for is Meteor, which has been enjoying steady downloads and GitHub stars. It integrates well with React and Angular and has plenty of nifty features. As a lightweight, full-stack JavaScript framework, developers are finding the Meteor framework a pleasure to work with. Meteor, always known as a solid beginner framework is great for prototyping as well.

The thing that has prevented Meteor from becoming a mainstream success is due to the hidden complexities that keep cropping up over time particularly when production is concerned. Meteor, despite having raised loads of money, isn't backed by a leading tech enterprise with a broad pool of engineers, like what React & AngularJS are. Notwithstanding the fact that AngularJS has plenty of issues and yet is backed up by Google, Meteor, on the other hand, is considered an investment risk as it's a framework for both the backend and frontend development. To get the most out of the deployment ease, Meteor would also need to be hosted.

Another thing that isn't working for Meteor at the moment is that many developers aren't big fans of the MongoDB and well, Mongo is Meteor's default database. Meteor will remain a nice though for 2017 since more developers will likely wait for more reliable evidence that Meteor can be used for large and more complex application development. Needless to say, Meteor will likely remain niche going forward in 2016 or even 2017. Most professional developers will wait for any evidence that it can be used for developing large, complex applications.

ES6 At Last

One of the things that JavaScript developers do in 2016 moving forward 2017 is to ensure that all their apps are ES2015 compliant. But like many other complications with tech apps and programming language, we have the Babel vs. TypeScript issue.

Babel mostly translates the ES6 code to ES5 whereas TypeScript is really a superset of JavaScript that adds necessary but optional static typing to JavaScript and then compiles all of this to plain JavaScript as well. Babel and TypeScript have been created with totally different purposes and therefore not comparable.

Babel, developed by Facebook, supports Flow which also adds in the static type-checking for JavaScript. Using Babel makes a little bit more sense since you can use both consecutively. Babel was also the first to helped bridge the difference between ES5 and ES6 applications.

TypeScript on the other hand only supports ES6, thus playing second fiddle to Babel when it comes to progressiveness. Checking in with the GitHub stars, it looks like Babel is the most preferred transpiler. React developers also prefer to use the Babel + Webpack combo.

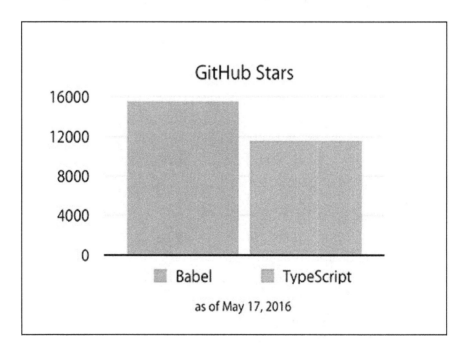

Despite the stars, TypeScript seems to be a lot more viable and sometimes and even preferred choice especially if you are looking for a solution to make your JavaScript codebase much more manageable. JavaScript has always been known to be a difficult to read language making it even more difficult to debug, due to its weak type-checking system. So in terms of support, TypeScript has enjoyed a larger following than Flow.

The graph below shows the Google Trends Graph showing the growth of interest for TypeScript.

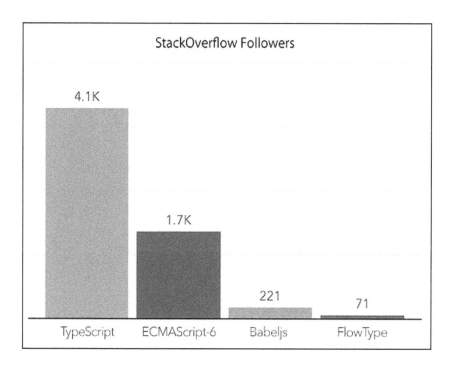

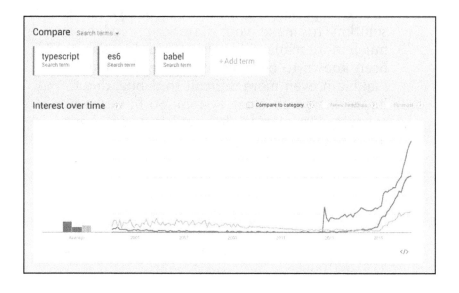

Another reason that TypeScript could be getting popular is because of Angular2, but just because JavaScript apps get larger focus, that isn't the contributing reason of why TypeScript becomes popular.

While Redux has made testing much easier, TypeScript makes codebase a lot easier to maintain. Apart from this, Google, Facebook, and Microsoft are collaborating to add on static typing to JavaScript and thus paving the way to EMCAScript.

At the same time, Google dropped AtScript and AngularJS in favor for TypeScript by Microsoft. Flow by Facebook, on the other hand, doesn't have the same community popularity as TypeScript.

This goes to show that statically typed JavaScript is an active and growing trend that even JavaScript non-believers will approve of where is TypeScript is the most solid solution.

Functional Programming is Becoming Mainstream

Plenty of functional programming platforms have been making their way into mainstream programming but very recently, the 'functional programming model' has gained plenty of attention especially with the rise of complex web apps.

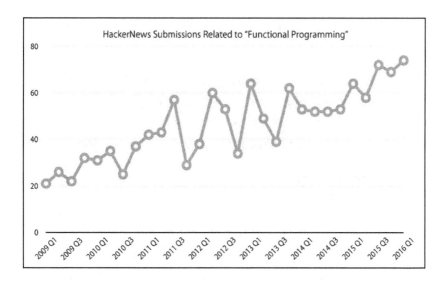

HackerNews Submissions Related to "Functional Programming"

Scala is coming back as a favored language among backend developers who want to embrace functional programming. However, Facebook's React, on the other hand, has encouraged front-end JavaScript developers to take on UI development using a practical approach.

More and more positive feedback is coming in for functional programming, and it looks like it will become mainstream in 2017. At this point of time, front-end web development is taking the forefront in reactive and functional programming.

So the React+Redux agenda is really the most sought after beginner-friendly solution for those that are comfortable with programming that is object-oriented. In other words, React only needs developers to take a functional approach to UI whereas Redux is mostly a system that encourages a practical approach to handling data. All other things are done in the OOP-style.

RxJS

But for those who still want to go on track with the full-on functional reactive programming, which is considered the 'true' FRP and still want to use JavaScript, then RxJS is a necessary skill to learn. RxJS is an extension of JavaScript that is reactive that can be used to replace the Flux architecture. It may sound like overkill for simple and small apps but in truth, it builds a powerful foundation for web applications that will go through a complicated stream of processing.

Netflix uses RxJS while Angular2 also relies on RxJS. Developed by Microsoft, RxJS works incredibly well with TypeScript thus developers can expect that RxJS will continue to be improved.

Learning RxJS though is an entirely different arena. It has a steep learning curve that make most developers give up on doing any FRP in JavaScript and pick up other functional programming languages that are compatible with JavaScript.

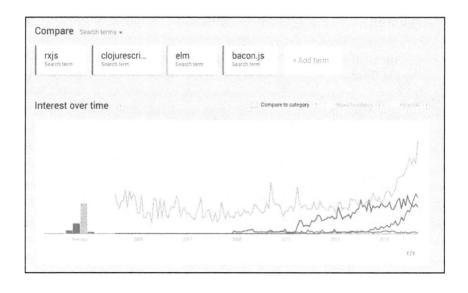

Some of the compatible programming that developers choose to use instead of RxJS is ClojureScript and Elm. However all these program's growth and popularity pales in comparison with Redux+React.

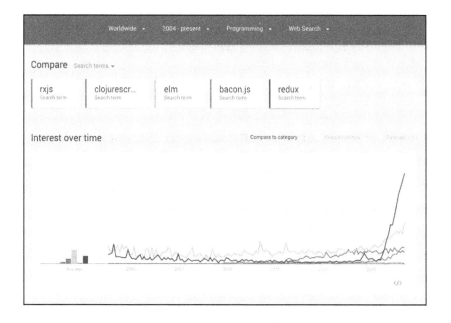

The thing is, looking at how functional programming fits perfectly with addressing modern issues in web development, one has to agree that functional programming paradigm and its equivalent concepts will stick around as a necessary skill that JavaScript developers will need to harness and learn.

Desktop Framework Showdown: Nw.js vs. Electron

Plenty of data nowadays requires synchronizing data from various platforms such a desktop and mobile. However, many services mostly start out as web apps before they are converted as desktop apps for enhanced user-experience. It is done this way because web app developments are a lot faster and more easily updated. Above all, users can also try out web apps more instantly without having to install anything else.

Developers in the past were confined to using CEF if they wanted to use web technologies to create front-end UI for desktop apps. Not an easy process and the apps themselves weren't truly cross-platform compatible. Though that, Node.js has made cross-platform apps easier for desktop frameworks. The shift of using web technologies for desktop app development began to rise starting 2014.

Thus, let's take a look at the GitHub Star history for both projects:

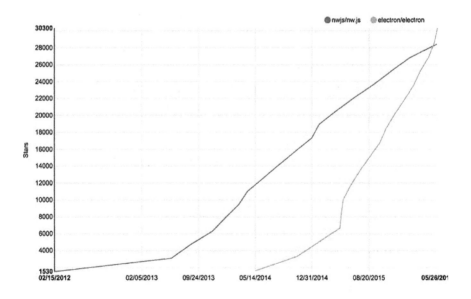

Although Nw.js broke into the scene much earlier and is considered older, it looks like Electron is growing at an explosive rate, while nw.js is growing at a monotonous linear rate.

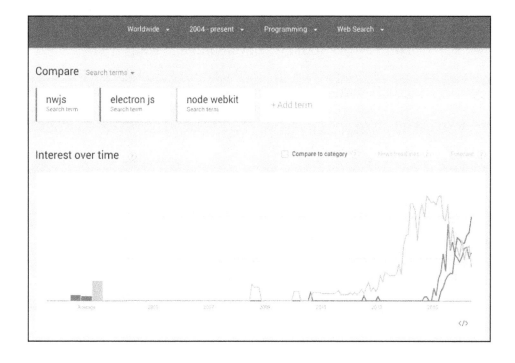

While Electron is pretty new, it is used by several established organizations like Slack, Microsoft (Visual Studio Code), WordPress, and Sencha. But with the ease of use that Electron's has, the network and community grew very fast. This wave of popularity is very likely to go on into 2017, thus enabling

Electron to become the framework of choice for desktop and web app development.

Mobile App Framework Showdown: React Native vs. Ionic

When Reactive Native came out, it was predicted that it would take over and charts the course of mobile development with web technologies since it can be used to develop cross-platform apps natively. So is 2017 the year of React Native? There might be some expectations to that through this graph:

At this moment, React Native has not yet released any updated software as it is still at version 0.26. Whether or not it will become mainstream in 2017 depends largely on developer's patience to deal with app-development changes that needs refactoring the whole codebase together with other issues.

Therefore, let's take a look at the approximate

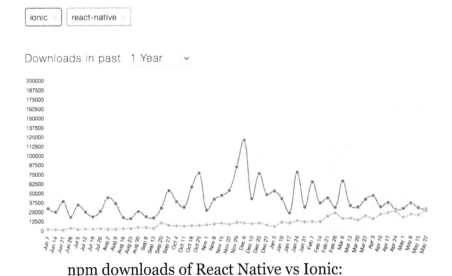

npm downloads of React Native vs Ionic:

From the graph, it seems that React Native is on track to overtake ionic as the framework of choice for cross-platform mobile development using web technologies.

In terms of the job market, React Native is also becoming more in-demand than Ionic:

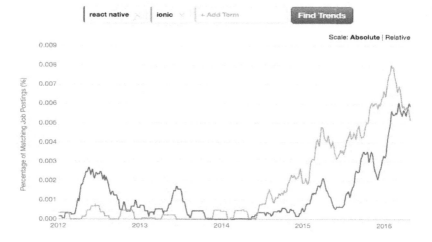

| react native | ionic | + Add Term | Find Trends |

A quick search on job postings, show that at least 75 job postings are looking for developers with ionic skills whereas 65 job postings are looking for developers with React skills. This shows that there is an increasing surge of the familiarity with React Native that will most likely be a huge push to any up and coming developers going forward 2017.

The Future of Web API: GraphQL vs REST

Soon after Facebook mentioned that they were open-sourcing GraphQL, plenty of JavaScript developers jumped onto the hype train earlier on in 2016, especially since Facebook turned into the Apple of JavaScript when it came to open source projects.

GraphQL was aiming to sort of replace REST APIs, but considering how ubiquitous REST APIs are, this is an unlikely scenario:

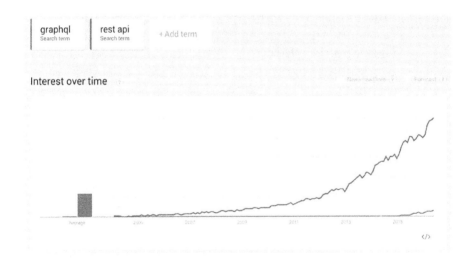

GraphQL would do well with REST APIs, but it will definitely not replace REST as some developers thought it would have. Even more to do with this is that GraphQL is relatively new and linked with Facebook Relay, so there aren't any learning resources or best practices for programmers and developers to pick the skill up elsewhere. With that said, 2017 is still too early for GraphQL to be going mainstream despite the strong hype it has now.

JavaScript Trends Conclusion

In conclusion, the community of JavaScript moves and changes at a fast pace, keeping up with any upcoming trends and in line with mainstream technology which means more support, relevance, and resources. Based on the trends discussed in this chapter, JavaScript developers should equip themselves with Redux & React and also with other familiar functional programming such as TypeScript. Not only that, having experience with React Native and Electron will definitely give upcoming programmers a lot more push and credibility in a job search.

Conclusion

Thank for making it through to the end of *JavaScript: Tips and Tricks to Programming Code with JavaScript*. Let's hope it was informative and able to provide you with all of the tools you need to achieve your goals whatever it may be.

The next step is to use the coding skills that you have learned and apply it to your own projects. Learning takes time, but you should be patient because just like when you learn anything new, you are going to make mistakes.

Go over the lessons in this book again and reread them. Learning how to write code is going to be confusing until you get the hang of it because of all the different conditions and exceptions that you are going to learn.

Finally, if you found this book useful in anyway, a review on Amazon is always appreciated!